MINOTAUR

OTHER BOOKS BY SERPENT CLUB PRESS:

What Was Left of the Stars
Claire Åkebrand

Circumambulate
Daniel Bossert

A Quarter Century
Eda Gasda

Moon on Water
Sonata for Piano and Violin
Matthew Gasda

Autumn, Again; Spring, Anew
Michael Skelton & Stephen Morel

The Substitute
Michael Skelton

On Bicycling: An Introduction
Samuel Atticus Steffen

AND OUR JOURNAL
New Writing: Volume I
New Writing: Volume II

MINOTAUR
A play by Matthew Gasda

MINOTAUR
Copyright © Serpent Club Press, 2017
All rights reserved

No part of this book may be used or reproduced in any manner whatsoever without written permission except in the case of brief quotations embodied in critical articles and reviews.

The scanning, uploading and distribution of this book via the Internet or via any other means without permission of the publisher is illegal and punishable by law.
For more information please contact Serpent Club Press at editor@serpentclub.org

Serpent Club Press books may be purchased for educational, business, or sales promotional use.
For more information please contact Serpent Club Press at editor@serpentclub.org

CAUTION: Professionals and amateurs are herby warned that all material in this book, being fully protected under the copyright laws of the United States of America, and all the other countries of the Copyright Union, is subject to royalty. All rights, including professional, amateur, motion picture, recitation, lecturing, public reading, radio and television broadcasting, and the rights of translation into foriegn languages are strictly reserved.

ALL INQUIRIES concerning performance rights for the plays in this volume should be addressed to editor@serpentclub.org

First Edition

Printed in the United States of America
Set in Williams Caslon
Designed by Emily Gasda

ISBN
9780997613452

MINOTAUR

MINOTAUR had its world premiere at Arts on Site on September 13, 2017 (Shelby Phillips, Producer). It was directed by Matthew Gasda; the costume and set design was by Theresa Zeitz-Lindamood. The dramaturg was Kelly Swope, and the stage manager was Joanna Pisano. The cast was as follows:

Maud	Hannah McKechnie
Clara	Melissa Rae Nelson
Doug	Bruce Barton
Edith	Katherine Wessling
Theo	Ryan Feyk

Characters:

MAUD, a professional, 27
CLARA, a writer, sister to Maud, 23
DOUG, an architect, Clara and Maud's father, 60
EDITH, a lawyer, Doug's wife and stepmother to Maud and Clara, 50
THEO, a filmmaker, Edith's son from another marriage, 31

Setting:

Christmas Eve in a well-to-do, secluded house during a snowstorm.

ACT I
SCENE 1

A bathroom, with a bathtub.

Clara takes a bubble bath and drinks a glass of wine. Her sister Maud sits against the door. Maud is also drinking wine.

Maud gets up and opens the window and puts her wine glass on the windowsill. Maud takes a cigarette from her shirt pocket.

CLARA
Edith is gonna kill us.

MAUD
She's not going to find out—

Enter Edith.

EDITH
Sorry to bother you both. I thought you might need a fresh towel Clara. And girls, please, please don't smoke in here. You know it drives me crazy.

CLARA
Thanks Edith.

Exit Edith.

CLARA
You were saying?

Maud lights her cigarette.

MAUD
Whatever.

CLARA
Can you hand me my phone?

MAUD
Why are we not at the hospital with Pop-Pop?

CLARA
Because.

MAUD
I wish he and Dad would just like, forgive each other.

CLARA
It's not gonna happen at this point.

MAUD
Why not?

CLARA
Because it just won't. Here, take my phone back, I don't want it to get sudsy.

MAUD
You live on that thing.

CLARA
Are you gonna tell Edith and Dad about the engagement?

MAUD
I don't know.

CLARA
It's awkward right?—having to convince people of something you've not convinced yourself of…

MAUD
Just because your love-life is a mess—

CLARA
If you're implying that I'm jealous: no; fuck no, I'm not—

MAUD
You've been acting like it.

CLARA
How so?

MAUD
You've been persistently unkind.

CLARA
You think I'm trying to make you feel as shitty about yourself as I feel about myself?

MAUD
You like that I'm miserable…

CLARA
Can you hand me my phone again?

MAUD
No.

CLARA
Why not?

MAUD
You need to disconnect.

CLARA
Gimme the phone dude.

MAUD
One bathtub selfie is enough.

CLARA
Not for my followers.

MAUD
It's so gross, the way you scrape together a meaningful image from meaningless experiences. Like, just because you went to Vassar and became a situational lesbian doesn't mean—

CLARA
I'm sorry, what?

MAUD
I mean, like; haunting literary parties, getting a book deal to write about yourself—

CLARA
First of all, you're one to talk; especially about situational lesbianism—

MAUD
Excuse me?

CLARA
In high school? Those so-called sleepovers—

MAUD
That doesn't count—

CLARA
And second of all, you don't even read my writing—

MAUD
Because I like to keep my food down—

CLARA
You didn't use to.

MAUD
Another cheap shot!

CLARA
I feel like you and Edith are friends.

MAUD
I like Edith.

CLARA
Dad told me he wants to get an apartment in the city; just for himself.

MAUD
That's kind of a bad sign?

CLARA
It is for Edith—

MAUD
They seem happy though.

CLARA
'Seem.'

MAUD
You refuse to see the good in people—

CLARA
You refuse to see anything other than the good in people—

MAUD
It makes me really sad to talk to you sometimes.

CLARA
Just be glad that you're not me and move on.

MAUD
I admire you.

CLARA
Mistakenly.

MAUD
I just can't keep up with you sometimes.

CLARA
You can't let so much of the world in. It's too exhausting.

MAUD
It hurts me that you don't admire me the way I admire you.

CLARA
Don't court my approval, please.

MAUD
I want to be friends.

CLARA
Friendship is so banal.

MAUD
We used to be close—

CLARA
When we were little children—

MAUD
There's a bond—

CLARA
No, there's guilt over the lack of a bond.

MAUD
Guilt is a kind of bond.

CLARA
Guilt is a very profound form of torture.

MAUD
Clara—

CLARA
What?

MAUD
I love you.

CLARA
I got a text—

Maud looks at the phone.

MAUD
Someone named Sarah Nicole—

CLARA
My editor—give it here; please don't read it.

MAUD
I'm not, chill.

Maud hands Clara the phone.

MAUD
You're in love with her—

CLARA
Vaguely.

MAUD
Honestly, can you just tell me once and for all if you're really a dyke?

CLARA
No.

MAUD
No as in you're not or no as in you won't tell me?

CLARA
No as in go fuck yourself.

MAUD
You're so weird.

CLARA
You're afraid of anything that violates the little moral paradigm you've built with super-glue, tape, and Catholic guilt.

MAUD
I've not, for a single second of my life, felt safe.

CLARA
So let's talk about that: your not feeling safe.

MAUD
Because I'm not really talking to you, Clara; I'm talking to "Clara" the gossip columnist, the internet personality, the erotic self-help writer—

CLARA
Clara the third-rate hack is as much a performance as Maud the first-rate Hausfrau.

MAUD
> I can't deal with people who sound so sure of themselves when I don't feel sure of anything.

CLARA
> Sounding sure is not being sure—

MAUD
> I know.

CLARA
> Because neither of us are sure about anything—

MAUD
> I know.

CLARA
> Can you just give me my phone?

> *Maud takes the phone and tosses into the tub, where it lands with a plop. Clara frantically tries to save it.*

CLARA
> I could have been electrocuted.

MAUD
> I doubt it.

CLARA
> Are you gonna buy me a new one?

MAUD
> I doubt it.

CLARA
> You're unbelievable.

MAUD
> Have Dad get you a new one.

CLARA
> Now I have no connection to the outside world. When I go literally insane, you have only yourself to blame.

MAUD
> How will I live with myself?

CLARA
The same way you always do: with the overwhelming force of self-deception.

MAUD
That's not fair—

CLARA
Of course it is. For instance: explain to me why you're getting married to a closeted investment banker—

MAUD
Look—

CLARA
I know, I know: you love each other—

MAUD
But we do!

CLARA
You mean: you like the same interior decorating catalogues.

MAUD
Stop making assumptions.

CLARA
Is it that you feel more attractive when he makes you dress up a boy?

MAUD
Oh my god stop—

CLARA
I'm having too much fun.

MAUD
Pop-Pop asked me this morning why we don't visit him more often.

CLARA
I don't like doing things just for the sake of doing them.

MAUD
He's dying—

CLARA
Everyone's dying.

MAUD
He's scared. He's alone.

CLARA
　Everyone's scared. Everyone's alone.

MAUD
　You know what I mean.

CLARA
　Death-bed selfies do not fit my Instagram aesthetic.

MAUD
　In a few days, he's gonna be gone forever.

CLARA
　And in the scheme of eternity, it will not matter if I visited him for two hours before he died.

MAUD
　But in the scheme of his life, it will.

CLARA
　Hey, we should put my phone in a bowl of rice.

MAUD
　Fuck your phone.

CLARA
　Why are you so cunty? Honestly—

MAUD
　You know, before I met Marco I drank myself to sleep every night.

　Enter Edith.

EDITH
　I'm sorry, I couldn't help but overhear.

MAUD
　Overhear what exactly?

CLARA
　How long were you at the door?

EDITH
　Just a few minutes—

CLARA
　Fantastic.

EDITH
I already put some rice on the stove. OH MY GOD—I put rice on the stove!

Exit Edith.

CLARA
I hate this house.

MAUD
It's cozy.

CLARA
I've never been able to break it to Dad that I don't like his buildings.

MAUD
They're not that bad.

CLARA
They're actually kind of frightening.

MAUD
They're cold.

CLARA
Edith didn't need to actually have to steam the rice, the point is to put the phone in rice that will absorb the water. Whatever.

MAUD
Now Edith thinks that Marco's gay and that I'm an alcoholic.

CLARA
He is gay. You are an alcoholic.

MAUD
You don't know him.

CLARA
I've met him—

MAUD
In passing—

CLARA
Which was all the evidence I needed.

MAUD
You're poisonous.

CLARA
You're dramatic.

MAUD
Out of curiosity—how often do you masturbate?

CLARA
What do you think I'd be doing if you'd get out of the fucking bathroom?

MAUD
I mean, I'm trying to avoid cocktail hour.

CLARA
Cocktail hour is the worst.

MAUD
Exactly. Which is why I'd rather fight with you in here—

CLARA
We're not fighting.

MAUD
Have you ever considered that your interpretation of how the world works is not the only one?

CLARA
I mean, I've considered it—

MAUD
You don't realize how much I have to apologize to other people for your behavior—

CLARA
That's just your own sense of shame and propriety kicking in.

MAUD
You get off when you write something controversial and the internet blows up—

CLARA
Why don't we just live and let live?

MAUD
You say 'live and let live' after spending the whole day criticizing me.

CLARA
Consistency is the hobgoblin of little minds.

MAUD
Consistency is sanity.

CLARA
Just leave the bathroom Maud—

MAUD
I can't.

CLARA
Why not?

MAUD
Because you won't admit that you're vulnerable; you won't be vulnerable.

CLARA
So what?

MAUD
I'm tired of this loafer posture; this veneer of I-don't-really-need-this, while privately being desperate for this, whatever this is.

CLARA
I don't get it.

MAUD
Just say that life hurts you too.

CLARA
Put your finger here; see my hands. Reach out your hand and put it into my side. Stop doubting and believe.

MAUD
I'm serious…

CLARA
Of course life hurts me Maud. Of course it does. It hurts me so consistently—so divinely—that I walk around in a state of nervous shock. I'm just good at hiding it.

MAUD
Then why do you act like nothing bothers you?

CLARA
I don't, I act like you don't bother me.

MAUD
I want to know that you're listening when I speak.

CLARA
You want to have the power to make me feel like shit.

MAUD
Because you make me feel like shit—

CLARA
No, I just point out the ways in which you intentionally prevent yourself from taking any real risks in life—

MAUD
I don't intentionally do anything—

CLARA
Which is precisely your problem.

MAUD
But not yours…

CLARA
Oh no: I'm very intentional. For instance, I feel like the best life hack for me is only dating like, 40-year-old male creatives obsessed with their careers. They slot me in from time to time, which fits my schedule perfectly, and they share my goals when it comes to optimal socializing.

MAUD
But that sounds horrible—

CLARA
Half a woman's life is wasted splurging to help and console others. But men don't do that, which is admirable. So I want to be more like them, rather than less.

MAUD
Empty and self-satisfied?

CLARA
Ideally.

MAUD
Sometimes I can't listen to you talk. It's just verbal Instagram; like why even use words?

CLARA
I'm thinking about Mom.

MAUD
Oh.

CLARA
She was the last person to die in the family. I just realized. My feet are getting cold.

MAUD
Get out then—

CLARA
No, I'm comfortable.

MAUD
Mom used to take long baths too.

CLARA
I know. This bath is an homage.

MAUD
Clara…

CLARA
I can't believe you don't think I show vulnerability.

MAUD
Missing Mom isn't being vulnerable.

CLARA
Yes it is.

MAUD
No, missing Mom is missing Mom. Being vulnerable is something else.

CLARA
What is being vulnerable then?

MAUD
Being vulnerable means being able to accept pity from someone else.

CLARA
That's such bullshit.

MAUD
Why? Explain?

CLARA
I used to fall asleep reading a book, now I fall asleep looking at my phone.

MAUD
Do you really think Marco's gay?

CLARA
Don't you?

MAUD
It's not that simple.

CLARA
I know.

MAUD
You want to start unravelling little bits of me without really wanting to do justice to the whole picture—

CLARA
You go to the dog park in the mornings, after coffee, then you come back and have eggs and a little endive salad. Always endive. It's so decadent. And then Marco wakes up and you talk and he gets ready for work and you get ready for work and he jacks off to the sight of construction workers jackhammering outside. There, that's the whole picture.

MAUD
We wanna have kids.

CLARA
Matrimony is like setting up a limited liability corporation for the enterprise of procreation.

MAUD
I want little children who scamper across hardwood floors in bare feet; I want a dog who barks at the mailman. I want to go to parent-teacher conferences and hear how gifted my children are.

CLARA
I don't.

MAUD
But I wonder if I'm trying to compensate for our childhood being essentially a failure…

CLARA
It think it's a safe bet that that's exactly what you're doing.

MAUD
The winter Mom died was especially lovely. Do you remember that? How clear and cold the days were; how slowly they moved, like birds through empty air—

CLARA
I made a mistake bringing Mom up, let's just not go there right now. Ok?

MAUD
It's really frustrating that you just want to cut yourself off from our past—

CLARA
All we do in this family—I mean all you and Dad and I do—is talk about Mom. It's our only leitmotif. I'm sorry that she got in a car accident. I'm sorry that she was so wonderful. But Christ, I can't imagine that she would have wanted us to spend our whole lives building a shrine to her existence. Mom was a fucking free-spirit. Like the freest. She wore crazy clothes, did drugs, fucked a lot of guys before Dad and probably a lot after him too. And then she disappeared forever. I don't know what to say. I mean, do you think I love her any less than you do?

MAUD
That's not what I'm saying—

CLARA
Because I feel like it is—

MAUD
Don't get upset—

CLARA
Don't get upset!

MAUD
I mean—

CLARA
Of course I'm gonna get upset!

Enter Edith carrying a bowl of steaming rice.

MAUD
Edith, I'm sorry, but can you not barge in?

CLARA
It's an absurdist routine—

EDITH
Sorry! I have the rice—

CLARA
Oh, the great, the pointless, the sacred rice bowl; bring it to me—

EDITH
And I, um, I wanted to tell you that Theo called: he said he's decided to drive up for dinner tonight.

MAUD
Tonight?

EDITH
Yes. As we speak. I have an impetuous son. So the two of you should probably get dressed. We're going to sit down for dinner in an hour or so, and your father has started talking about going to midnight mass.

CLARA
Mass?

EDITH
I think with your Pop-Pop beginning to fade…

CLARA
Ok ok. Edith can you close the door now?

EDITH
Yes. I'm just letting you know. Ok? Hurry up please!

CLARA
Thanks for the head's up. So so much. Now go away. Thank you. Bye. Buh bye. Bye bye.

Exit Edith.

MAUD
It's been so long since we saw Theo.

CLARA
A few years.

MAUD
Crazy.

CLARA
I guess.

MAUD
I don't want to go to mass.

CLARA
Then don't go.

MAUD
But we have to—

CLARA
No we don't.

MAUD
If Dad wants to—

CLARA
We can do whatever we want.

MAUD
Then why do I feel constrained?

CLARA
Because you believe that constraining yourself is an act of kindness.

MAUD
There are better, more interesting words than kindness: sympathy, moral imagination, a listening spirit.

CLARA
You're afraid of being selfish. Afraid having a self to be selfish with.

MAUD
Do you in fact want forgiveness? Do you think you've done something wrong? Are you sorry? If so, an apology is in order: a true one-one that names the fault, and the reason the fault is a fault, as well as an intention to do differently, slash better, in the future...

CLARA
Excuse me Maud, but what the fuck are you talking about?

MAUD
Refusing to go to the hospital the day Mom died.

CLARA
I was so young.

MAUD
Nevertheless, I'm asking: do you want forgiveness?

CLARA
Not right now thanks.

MAUD
Are you sure?

CLARA
You know, I think that privately, you resent Edith. I think you imagine Dad would be happier if he relied more on you than her.

MAUD
That's enough.

CLARA
Just tell me why you're getting married—

MAUD
Why does there need to be a reason?

CLARA
Good answer. Can you get my towel for me?

MAUD
Not right now. I feel like I might like to see you laugh; like really really laugh in a totally non-sarcastic, non-ironic, anti-Byronic, unselfconscious sort of way—

CLARA
Eh.

MAUD
I think I've see you do this maybe three times in your whole life—

CLARA
Everybody makes mistakes.

MAUD
You refuse to acknowledge that you have the same problems you point out in other people—

CLARA
I acknowledge my weaknesses all the time; constantly in fact—

MAUD
But you don't feel to other people like you do.

CLARA
That's not my problem. I wonder if my phone's ok—

MAUD
Relax.

CLARA
I am relaxed.

MAUD
You're anxious.

CLARA
You're making me anxious—

MAUD
Sorry.

CLARA
Why are you so fidgety all of a sudden?

MAUD
It's funny, I don't believe in life after death, but I believe in a life after death for Mom.

CLARA
Me too.

MAUD
It doesn't make any sense.

CLARA
No, it doesn't.

MAUD
It's a lie though—

CLARA
It's the only thing we've said tonight that's true.

MAUD
Maybe.

CLARA
You know, every therapist I've had has loved me. My therapists weep and mourn after we part, keep tabs on me for years to come, as if they don't want to lose touch with this phenomenal fount of candor. Give me my towel—

MAUD
Once I finish this cigarette.

CLARA
Now you're ruffling through pages and pages of memory. I can hear it.

MAUD
Put your hands over your ears.

CLARA
Metaphysical ears can't be closed.

MAUD
Metaphysical ears?

CLARA
As in: ears that hear souls in pain.

MAUD
Oh. Church is going to be so gloomy tonight.

CLARA
Pop-Pop won't be alive when we wake up.

MAUD
Death is like a fire in the room; or an animal—it speaks, hollers, barks, growls back at me.

CLARA
My feet are cold. Can you please get my towel?

MAUD
Fine.

Maud hands Clara the towel.

Exit Clara.

Exit Maud.

ACT I
SCENE 2

Edith smokes pensively at the bathroom window. She is dressed for church.

Enter Clara, also dressed for church.

CLARA
Jesus Christ, Edith. I have to pee. Are you smoking?

EDITH
What does it look like I'm doing?

CLARA
Smoking.

EDITH
So there ya go.

CLARA
You're pleasantly surprising—

EDITH
You want one?

CLARA
Sure, why not? Mass tonight was eerie. It's been a hot minute since I've been to church. By which I mean, like, a decade.

EDITH
You think I'm surprising?

CLARA
I always knew you were, but now I have proof.

EDITH
No one ever asks me about myself—

CLARA
I bet Maud does—

EDITH
Yes, but she never actually listens to the answer.

CLARA
No, she never does.

EDITH
I learned when I was still young, that I was intelligent enough to take a lot of risks. And so I did. And still do.

CLARA
You pretend to be everybody's ally, but you're really nobody's ally; you're on your own side—

EDITH
You pretend not to be anyone's ally, but you're secretly allied to everyone.

CLARA
Maybe.

EDITH
Everyone in this family complains about loneliness, but you're the only one, I think, who's actually alone.

CLARA
Maybe.

EDITH
You never make eye-contact when you talk to people.

CLARA
Correction: when I talk to some people.

EDITH
When you talk to me—

CLARA
No, never.

EDITH
Why?

CLARA
Maud is on her way to becoming you, by the way.

EDITH
And that bothers you?

CLARA
She accepted you, let you in. She was infiltrated.

EDITH
And you resisted—

CLARA
The work of love is remembering one who is dead.

EDITH
I'm not her, I've never pretended I could replace her—

CLARA
I never asked to have you in my life—

EDITH
Frankly, I never asked to have you in mine; but you were part of the deal.

CLARA
I wish I'd had more say in the matter.

EDITH
It must be difficult to be so passionate Clara. I'm sorry.

CLARA
I'm sure you are.

EDITH
I respect you Clara.

CLARA
Ew.

EDITH
You don't have to believe me.

CLARA
I don't want to believe you.

EDITH
Whatever you say.

CLARA
I'm surrounded by people who have nothing to do but like fret over which brand of coconut oil to buy and which alternative gender word to use for the boy or girl who fucks them. People who think being caught up on Netflix is being cultured. I still have to pee. Can you leave now?

EDITH
Merry Christmas Clara.

Exit Edith.

ACT I
SCENE 3

Enter Maud and Theo.

MAUD
We're gonna wake the whole house up.

THEO
Who cares?

MAUD
I wish we could just talk for once.

THEO
No you don't.

MAUD
I'm standing here thinking, 'I love this person.'

THEO
Cool.

MAUD
I scare myself when I'm with you.

THEO
I'm not sure what you mean by that.

MAUD
I want you to read me, not fuck me—

THEO
I don't see the point—

MAUD
The heart is a book of luminous things.

THEO
The heart is a machine-part.

MAUD
There are layers.

THEO
To what?

MAUD
To me. The first layer is silence. The second layer: an endless profusion of profound words. The third layer: sentimentality. The fourth layer: honesty.

THEO
I don't know what you're talking about. All I could think about on the drive up was the taste of your skin.

MAUD
Go away.

THEO
I'm a part of your life.

MAUD
I feel like I've been flayed.

THEO
You talk about being turned on like it's a religious experience.

MAUD
I mean—

THEO
Get up.

MAUD
Why? Come up. Let's do it. I'm ready. Come on. Fuck me.

THEO
Please stand up.

MAUD
Fine.

THEO
Why don't we just talk?

MAUD
I find that suggestion to be rather disingenuous.

THEO
Fair.

MAUD
You were so graceful when you were absent from my life. But now that you're here, you just seem contorted and ugly.

THEO
Cool.

MAUD
Did I hurt you right there?

THEO
No.

MAUD
I can't seem to sufficiently hurt people. I wonder what I'm doing wrong.

THEO
Everything you say is an attempt to hurt yourself, that's why.

MAUD
It's pitiful.

THEO
A little bit.

MAUD
Goddamn.

THEO
Stop hiding your strength.

MAUD
Why?

THEO
Because it doesn't fool me anymore.

MAUD
I'm not trying to fool you, I'm trying to fool myself.

THEO
Why?

MAUD
Out of compassion for the people I would hurt if I stopped pretending to be weak.

THEO
You're not helping them though, by being this way—

MAUD
You should stop pretending to be strong, by the way, just like I should stop pretending to be weak.

THEO
It's very difficult to accept that I'm not going to make anything out of my life.

MAUD
That sounds like a self-fulfilling prophecy.

THEO
I used to have obscene self-confidence—

MAUD
And now?

THEO
It's settled into regular arrogance.

MAUD
Why did you stop responding to my texts?

THEO
You told me not to respond even if you tried to contact me. Remember?

MAUD
I didn't know what I wanted…

THEO
Me?

MAUD
YES.

THEO
It's not too late.

MAUD
I snuck into your room every night for two years. When you went to college, I would lay in your bed and masturbate. No joke. I would push my nose into your pillow, bury my head in your clothes…. You know I like sleeping with you. But I feel like you expect it. It makes me so angry that you expect it—

THEO
Your voice is like the feeling of the wind before it starts.

MAUD
My voice is a hysterical staccato.

THEO
Your voice is alotta things.

MAUD
I don't want desire.

THEO
I do.

MAUD
You're just a major episode in the rejection I have been undergoing my entire life: from my father all the way up to now.

THEO
You rejected me—

MAUD
The best defense is offense.

THEO
The best defense is indifference.

MAUD
I'm so bored.

THEO
I think I miss my younger self.

MAUD
Why? Because you never attained status higher than cute bartender? That's a pretty good status. I know some people would kill for that status.

THEO
Like your boyfriend?

MAUD
Fiance—

THEO
Shit.

MAUD
Are you jealous of him?

THEO
In theory.

MAUD
He makes a lot of money—

THEO
Don't turn him into a caricature.

MAUD
But that's what I like about him.

THEO
No.

MAUD
No?

THEO
That's just ridiculous.

MAUD
Why do we have better sex than we have with other people?

THEO
Because we've found a way to both be selfish at the same time.

MAUD
I can't decide whether you're a piece of shit, or whether I wish was getting married to you instead of someone else.

THEO
Why am I potentially a piece of shit?

MAUD
You went to college and had fucked other girls while I was stuck here, falling apart.

THEO
So what?

MAUD
What do you want?

THEO
Not to lose you, not yet.

MAUD
Ugh.

THEO
Wrong answer?

MAUD
Wrong and right.

THEO
Neither of us are ready to walk away; not really.

MAUD
Did it ever occur to you that if my mother hadn't died, I would have never met you?

THEO
Considering that my mother was the lawyer your father hired after the accident: yes, it has—

MAUD
I can't forgive myself for being ok with that trade-off.

THEO
I'm not convinced you care about any of the things you say you care about.

MAUD
You're such a jerk.

THEO
You like starting puzzles but not completing them.

MAUD
You're not a puzzle.

THEO
Why, because I don't hide the fact that I like—

MAUD
Because you don't change over time—

THEO
I don't?

MAUD
No. You were a bonerface when I met you and you're a bonerface now.

THEO
Uhuh.

MAUD
You're one of those guys who think he's deep because classical music makes you cry; you rewatch your old student films and secretly think that you were a misunderstood genius; you think of your life as a process of soul-making and you think of your lovers as creative muses in that life-long project. But they're just girls you meet on dating apps; your films were derivative and stupid; your emotions aren't original or even appealing. Really, you're just a guy who ascribes false value to his own dicking around.

THEO
Are you done?

MAUD
I could keep going.

THEO
Why don't you then?

MAUD
I feel satisfied.

THEO
And you didn't even need to get undressed—

MAUD
Don't act so hurt.

THEO
It's hard not to act hurt when you're actually hurt.

MAUD
You're fine.

THEO
No. I'm not.

MAUD
Cry baby.

THEO
A directionless person shouldn't find a direction this way—

MAUD
What way?

THEO
With violence of spirit.

MAUD
You're right.

THEO
It's ok.

MAUD
Don't forgive me.

THEO
I don't know what else to do.

MAUD
It's freezing in this fucking bathroom right now—

Maud opens the window.

MAUD
But I need a cigarette.

THEO
Ok.

Maud lights a cigarette and leans her head out the window.

MAUD
The stars are out.

Theo walks up to Maud, takes the cigarette from her hands, throws it in the bathtub, and kisses her.

They break apart.

MAUD
Now I have to light another one.

Maud lights another cigarette.

THEO
I feel like I'm condemned to drum my fingers while you make up your mind about me.

MAUD
I made up my mind when I was sixteen.

THEO
And what did you decide?

MAUD
That you were insurance against the condition of being alone.

THEO
Pass me that cigarette.

Maud passes Theo the cigarette.

MAUD
Someone told me recently that having faith in yourself means a constant readiness for surprise, but I think faith means knowing yourself so well that nothing that happens to you is surprising. And everything surprises me. The fact that I kissed you and the fact that I still want to and the fact that I know that I won't.

THEO
When you speak, everything that makes you angry goes an octave higher than everything you love and forms a chord: strange, dissonant, painfully lovely.

MAUD
Honestly, I still just feel like all you want to do is have sex.

THEO
You want me to take responsibility for what you want to do.

MAUD
It'd be nice.

THEO
Fuck that.

MAUD
I think Clara wants to seduce you. She kept looking over at you during the service.

THEO
I see.

MAUD
You should do it.

THEO
I don't think you know what you're saying.

MAUD
Words—

THEO
Words are turds. What are we even talking about?

MAUD
What do you want?

THEO
The emotional stakes lowered enough so that I can jump over them.

MAUD
Coward.

THEO
Obviously.

MAUD
You don't have to be real, you just have to fool me.

THEO
I'm trying!

MAUD
This is me rolling my eyes.

THEO
When I was a little kid, I had this neighbor—a kid my age—who died on the fourth of July because he swallowed a Roman Candle. He was trying to hold the firework between his teeth and was walking around, showing off, and he tripped and swallowed it. He died as stars spilled from the ruin of his throat.

MAUD
You've told me that story before.

THEO
Because we've been having the same conversation for ten years.

MAUD
How do we get out of the loop?

THEO
We could just switch roles: you play the sexual manipulator, and I play the victim.

MAUD
Ok great let's do it, I'd find that more interesting.

THEO
You were so graceful when you were absent from my life. But now that you're here, you just seem contorted and ugly.

MAUD
Cool.

THEO
I love Jesus, but I also love it when you spit in my mouth.

MAUD
I completely lack empathy, but I have a rad Tindr account.

THEO
Do you care about me? Do you love me? Love me.

MAUD
I'm half a person but a whole dick.

THEO
I like it when you humiliate me.

MAUD
It's so depressing when fucking turns into negotiating.

THEO
Fucking implies negotiating.

MAUD
Just take off your clothes bitch.

THEO
Ok. The more disgusting the more I like it.

MAUD
Alright. That's enough.

THEO
La di da.

MAUD
I don't want to be strangers.

THEO
Tell me why you're getting married again?

MAUD
Because I need you too much. I know that's what you want to hear—

THEO
When are you gonna go towards your pain instead of running from it?

MAUD
When are you?

THEO
Probably never.

MAUD
Then don't expect it of me.

THEO
I'll see you in the morning.

MAUD
Wait—

THEO
What?

MAUD
I met you inside a vacuum of shame; I'd like to meet you on the outside of that vacuum, in normal gravity.

THEO
Another time then.

MAUD
What about right now? We could just sit and talk. I'll get a bottle of wine from the cellar—

THEO
I'm not in the mood.

MAUD
No?

THEO
> Not any more.

MAUD
> Theo, I'm sorry.

THEO
> You didn't do anything.

MAUD
> I don't like the idea that I hurt you.

THEO
> There are worse things than being hurt.

> *Exit Theo.*

ACT II
SCENE 1

The kitchen. Early morning.

Doug and Theo sit at the kitchen table.

DOUG
I'd like to be your friend, Theo.

THEO
That's nice.

DOUG
But clearly I don't know how to go about it—

THEO
I think you're an ass.

DOUG
Well, the feeling's mutual.

THEO
You have no idea how to talk to me, do you?

DOUG
You haven't stepped foot in this house for two years—

THEO
Why would I?

DOUG
We care about you.

THEO
Who's we?

DOUG
Your mother and I. Maud and Clara.

THEO
You want me to feel responsible—

DOUG
For what exactly?

THEO
Nothing binding together.

DOUG
There's something so arrogant about you.

THEO
If meaninglessness becomes concentrated enough, it—it fuses into something else.

DOUG
Which is what?

THEO
There's no word for it.

DOUG
I know how difficult it is pursuing your art…

THEO
You made me take out loans to go to film school. Remember?

DOUG
Bitterness doesn't suit you.

THEO
You're half of a complete person and always have been. You just happen to have the convenient excuse of having had a vaguely tragic life.

DOUG
Don't take it too easy on me now…

THEO
I don't plan on it.

DOUG
I think you use charisma to mask the fact that you've never really stopped being a teenager—

THEO
It's nine in the morning. It feels like I've traveled light years to get here. All I can think about are the coffee-grounds I want to turn into coffee. So I apologize if I'm um, unpleasant.

DOUG
It's alright.

THEO
Is it?

DOUG
I don't know.

THEO
There's supposed to be a big snow-storm tonight.

DOUG
I know.

THEO
How's your dad?

DOUG
Still, you know, dying.

THEO
I'm sorry.

DOUG
He always loved attention. He was a great storyteller. Told wonderful, dirty jokes. He had this big belly laugh. Now he's dying like a stray dog.

THEO
I didn't know stray dogs had access to top-notch hospital care.

DOUG
Why are you such a pain in the ass?

THEO
He was very military, my Dad—as you know. I guess as an act of rebellion or defiance or some shit: my Mom getting married at 21—

DOUG
Do you still talk to your father?

THEO
Very occasionally.

DOUG
I'm not him—

THEO
But you're not what I need either.

DOUG
But you're admitting that you need something—

THEO
It'd be nice to have someone to go to for advice.

DOUG
We're a lot alike, you know—

THEO
It's highly unpleasant.

DOUG
In some ways at least—

THEO
We both lack a foundation for our attempts at living meaningfully.

DOUG
Fathers define truth, sons have to accept it, or be accused of rebelling.

THEO
Painting yourself as the crippled son of a charismatic ego-maniac or whatever. It's clever. It's a big open-mouthed cry for sympathy.

DOUG
It's hard not to want sympathy on the day your father is going to die.

THEO
I guess.

DOUG
Every time you visit, I feel like you're positioning yourself for your mother's sympathy.

THEO
Well who else is gonna give it to me?

DOUG
Do you need money?

THEO
Isn't it a little late for that kind of offer?

DOUG
I stand to inherit a fairly tangible sum…

THEO
You have no idea how angry this is making me.

DOUG
How much would you need to make a feature?

THEO
More than you can give me.

DOUG
But to get started—

THEO
More than you will give me—

DOUG
How do you know?

THEO
I imagine you became an architect only after it was clear to you that you'd never make it as a real artist.

DOUG
I was relieved when I had two girls. I didn't want a son.

THEO
Which is the reason we're having this conversation. You're trying to find a way to apologize to me for rejecting me before we were even introduced.

DOUG
I'm sorry for that. By the way.

THEO
Or maybe I've just tricked you into thinking that your own subconscious is more unkind than it really is.

DOUG
I don't think you're tricking me…

THEO
Which doesn't mean I'm not.

DOUG
Why would you?

THEO
Because I can.

DOUG
Oh.

THEO
It was really weird for me when I figured out that sexual love was the thing that was keeping you and Mom together.

DOUG
Isn't this uncomfortable for you to talk about?

THEO
I think you're increasingly uncomfortable with how increasingly comfortable I am.

DOUG
Probably.

THEO
I think I'm more detached than comfortable, actually. I feel like an animal hibernating in its burrow.

DOUG
Stick around for a day or two. Stay for the funeral. I think it'd be good for Clara and Maud. I think it'd be good for you.

THEO
I'll think about it.

DOUG
The three of you need each other.

THEO
No comment.

DOUG
Right.

THEO
What?

DOUG
Nothing.

THEO
I had the flu last week. I could feel myself getting sick after work, so I put on three sweaters, wool socks, and drank half a bottle of whiskey, and went under the covers and sweated it out. I remember lying in bed, in the dark, feeling dizzy—

DOUG
When it snows up here, you can almost hear the dead, gliding over the earth—

THEO
I had the uncanny feeling that I was falling. That I'd been cast out of my body.

DOUG
The older you get, the harder it gets to see into yourself.

THEO
Or do you mean: the more terrifying it gets—

DOUG
One day, I'll be the one dying, and you'll be the one figuring out what to do with all of your anger.

THEO
As if I'm not trying to do that now?

DOUG
The stakes are higher when it's down to a matter of hours.

THEO
You know that I won't give a damn, right? When it's you—

DOUG
It's easy to say that now.

THEO
You're a circumstance, not a person—

DOUG
What is this really about Theo?

THEO
I'm in a violent mood.

DOUG
I dreamt that my wife was alive last night.

THEO
Oh, I used to talk to her ghost all the time in the garden. There's so much pathos in being haunted. Eventually, I had to tell her to leave me alone. So pretty though.

DOUG
Please don't mock me.

THEO
Irony. Saying one thing while meaning the other. And you have no idea how to handle it.

DOUG
I want to talk about things that matter to me.

THEO
Well, so do I.

DOUG
What matters to you Theo?

THEO
I told you: turning coffee-grounds into coffee. And, like, sorting myself out.

DOUG
What do you need to sort out?

THEO
Eh. Who knows. I mean, I began some kind of um, process of withdrawal a long time ago and I'm trying to figure out where that process leads. Self-parody maybe. I'd speak entirely in riddles if I could.

DOUG
Why?

THEO
Why not?

DOUG
Because then you don't let anyone in.

THEO
Exactly.

DOUG
But people want to be let in.

THEO
Sucks for them.

DOUG
I really just think this family needs you.

THEO
That's funny.

DOUG
I don't see why.

THEO
You know what personality is? It's a desperate bargain for sanity and constancy. A trick to astonish the brain into coherence.

DOUG
I've always been told that I lack a strong personality.

THEO
Which might be your greatest strength Dougie.

DOUG
What I don't like about having a dishwasher is that you don't get to do the dishes yourself; I find doing dishes very relaxing. Sometimes I do the dishes by hand even though I don't have to. It's nice.

THEO
My Dad, before my parents got divorced, used to take like, a ton of home videos. When I was older, a teenager—right before I met you—I used to go back and rewatch the stuff my Dad shot. Images of me in the hospital, newborn, tubes running from my nose; my Mom cradling me. She looked so pure, so aware, so loving. I wanted to make films like that. I wanted to make innocent images. Somewhere along the line, I forgot how. I feel like I'm talking to myself—

DOUG
I'm listening—

THEO
Does Clara know she isn't your biological daughter?

DOUG
Excuse me?

THEO
The ghost told me. In the garden. Years ago. So I'm asking: does Clara know?

DOUG
> This conversation is over.

THEO
> Don't shoot the messenger.

DOUG
> Whatever you're trying to do right now, it's not appreciated.

THEO
> Iris confronted you with the facts of her rather extensive history of infidelity, you kicked her out, it was snowing, the roads were bad. So you've always blamed yourself, naturally.

DOUG
> How would you know that?

THEO
> I already told you—

DOUG
> But really, Theo, how would you know? Did your mother tell you?

THEO
> No, because you never told her.

DOUG
> No, I never did.

THEO
> So the question of how I know remains—

DOUG
> Where are you getting your information from?

THEO
> I'm a good guesser.

DOUG
> This is unbelievable.

THEO
> Ghosts or guesses—which is it?

DOUG
> This is all very strange. Have you shared your theory with your mother?

THEO
I've not shared it with anyone. Also: it's not a theory.

DOUG
Perhaps. Alright. Can you kindly leave the kitchen now, Theo?

THEO
Sure thing Doug.

DOUG
Thank you.

Exit Theo.

Enter Edith.

EDITH
Am I bothering you?

DOUG
No.

EDITH
How's your Dad?

DOUG
Either raving or dreaming. Nearly dead either way. Who knows. The hospital was quiet this morning. Only the nurses and I were awake. I don't think I've really slept in two days.

EDITH
You poor thing.

DOUG
I'm alright.

EDITH
I doubt the kids will be up before noon; I heard people moving around the house until God knows when.

DOUG
They aren't kids anymore.

EDITH
I still think of them as kids.

DOUG
I don't.

EDITH
How do you think of them then?

DOUG
Regular people, regular adults, to whom I happen to be related.

EDITH
Hm.

DOUG
I'm just in a bad mood—

EDITH
It's ok Doug.

DOUG
Or not even bad, per se; dark. I'm in a dark mood.

EDITH
It's understandable…

DOUG
I've wanted him to die my whole life.

EDITH
No you haven't—

DOUG
My dad's like a thin sludge spread over the glass of the world. I'd like it wiped off.

EDITH
Geeze.

DOUG
On the other hand, I'm not sure what it will be like looking through clear glass. There's supposed to be a blizzard tonight.

EDITH
What if we can't get to the hospital?

DOUG
I imagine that's what will happen.

EDITH
Doug…

DOUG
Yes?

EDITH
You'll regret it later, if you let things happen that way.

DOUG
I'm all about regrets; they add a certain fragrance to life, like shadow to sunlight.

EDITH
I don't find your mood right now particularly pleasant.

DOUG
Neither do I.

EDITH
It's Christmas—

DOUG
On Christmas Day, my Dad used to get particularly drunk and would inevitably find a reason to whip me with his belt. He'd hit my Mom when she'd try to stop him; also inevitably. It builds character, a good belting. Of course, it builds the wrong kind of character; but character nonetheless.

EDITH
I could't sleep last night; I kept thinking about Clara and Maud and how lost they seemed; and Theo too—and you. And I know I annoy all of you with how much I worry, but—

DOUG
Don't worry about worrying.

EDITH
I don't see how I can stop—

DOUG
When I had this house built, Iris was pregnant with Maud, and I had made enough money to not care about my father's point of view. I loved this little piece of woods, how quiet it was, how you couldn't hear any cars; how if you didn't look too far in either direction, it felt a little like living in a very old forest. I had a romanticized idea about family life; about togetherness. I wanted to be a better father than my father was—and I was; I know I was. I had to be. But.

EDITH
I know what you're thinking: you're thinking that your father should have died instead of her—

DOUG
My brain feels like a chalkboard that's just been erased.

EDITH
What did your Dad say to you at the hospital?

DOUG
It's not relevant.

EDITH
I doubt that—

DOUG
The more successful my father became, the more he went further and further off in the direction of being an outsider, mainly, in simple terms, of alcoholism. My mother was the opposite. Very together, figuring out how to get along; before she got cancer…I'm sorry—just give me a second—

EDITH
It's ok.

DOUG
Shit.

EDITH
It's really ok.

DOUG
Stop saying that word: 'ok'. You're making me crazy.

EDITH
Sorry.

DOUG
Stop saying that too.

EDITH
Ok.

DOUG
I said stop!

EDITH
Sorry! I mean!

DOUG
You're giving me a headache.

EDITH
You accuse me of needing to be angry, of needing to let things out, but it's you—you're the one who's overwhelmed—broken—by everything you're not saying—

DOUG
There's a reason you make more money than I do.

EDITH
I'm not sure if that's a compliment...

DOUG
It's not.

EDITH
Fuck off, Doug.

DOUG
When the girls were little, sometimes I'd just stand outside and watch everyone moving around inside the house—the house that I dreamed up and built—and I'd cry...and then I'd come inside and pretend like nothing unusual was going on. These small spaces of love open up so briefly that it's almost impossible to remember that they were ever there. I just feel so raw. I don't think I've ever felt so raw before.

EDITH
You don't have to be married to me if you don't want to be.

DOUG
Our life together is this kind of fiction that's developed parallel to everything that's real, hasn't it?

EDITH
I think you're right: I am angry.

DOUG
You've never blown me, by the way; not since the first night we met.

EDITH
Is that a complete thought, or do you expect me to draw conclusions for you?

DOUG
The conclusion's built in there, somewhere.

EDITH
I'd be fascinated to hear you articulate it—

DOUG
It's more aesthetic not to.

EDITH
It would have been easier if you had aged into one of those men who give up on erections for good.

DOUG
Easier for both of us—

EDITH
It's my way of caring for you.

DOUG
Yet the effect produced is not care.

EDITH
You're emotionally injured and you want attention; someone to stroke your forehead; but at the same time, that's the total opposite of what you want, so you feel like you're losing your mind.

DOUG
A little bit—

EDITH
Have you ever thought that maybe Iris wasn't as happy with you as you were with her?

DOUG
I've considered it, yes.

EDITH
Because, I'm just saying—

DOUG
That's not 'just saying'—

EDITH
I mean, you act like your first marriage was so incredibly ideal—

DOUG
Real love, no matter how flawed, is always ideal I think—

EDITH
Because you have this intense and very catholic love of beauty; so when a woman dies before her beauty's gone, it—

DOUG
You're jealous—

EDITH
Of course I'm jealous.

DOUG
It's a very crude thing to be jealous of the dead.

EDITH
Well, that's what I am: a crude, jealous, nagging housewife.

DOUG
But you're not a housewife—

EDITH
But I feel like one, I act like one, I dress like one—what difference does it make that I technically make more money than you do? That I'm more successful in my profession than you are in yours? What difference does it make if I act like your needs—emotional, spiritual, erotic—are the only ones that matter?

DOUG
None.

EDITH
Exactly.

DOUG
Why not confront me then—if you find living with me so repressive—why not say something?

EDITH
Clearly both of us are holding things back—

DOUG
So why can't we communicate?

EDITH
Because we don't care enough to justify communication.

DOUG
Do you really believe that?

EDITH
I'd just like to be content with the harvest of the everyday. I want small things. Achievable things. I'd like to have a better relationship with Clara and Maud. I'd like to retire soon. Life is more complicated than it is long; so if you don't learn to let go of things Doug, then—

DOUG
Then I'll what—

EDITH
Then you'll continue to be really, really confused and unhappy.

DOUG
I want nothing from you but to see you.

EDITH
Open your eyes—

DOUG
They're open—

EDITH
Needless to say, you're either blind or not looking in the right place.

DOUG
There is so much in us that demands a burial. So many dead things.

EDITH
I'm gonna say this one more time: if you want sympathy just take it and shut up; or ask for something more sincere; but don't ask me to split the difference between empathy and sympathy, because that's no fun.

DOUG
Married people repeat themselves: constantly—open the same wounds; tell the same bad jokes—

EDITH
It makes you wonder why there are any married people at all.

DOUG
Yeah. It does.

EDITH
It's like waiting for birds to return again in the spring—

DOUG
What is?

EDITH
Waiting for understanding.

DOUG
There's a certain violence in articulating exactly what you're feeling.

EDITH
Yes. There is.

DOUG
I want you to be direct with me.

EDITH
Direct? No, no. I don't see how that's possible.

DOUG
Why not?

EDITH
Because you're sad, desperate, absurd, and unrealistic.

DOUG
That sounded direct.

EDITH
Ok maybe it was.

DOUG
The feeling childhood left me with was one of humiliation.

EDITH
That's the feeling it leaves everyone with.

DOUG
Hmm.

EDITH
You don't think so?

DOUG
It's an uncomfortable thought.

EDITH
It's a realistic thought.

DOUG
Being at church last night brought back terrible memories. I don't know why I made everyone go.

EDITH
Because you wanted everyone to feel terrible—

DOUG
Yeah.

EDITH
Because you feel terrible.

DOUG
Empty—

EDITH
Or empty.

DOUG
Abandoned.

EDITH
Or abandoned.

DOUG
I'm going for a walk.

ACT II
SCENE 2

Afternoon. Maud and Edith sit together with a teapot between them.

EDITH
Why didn't you go to the hospital with everyone else?

MAUD
I stopped caring. And I guess Clara started.

EDITH
Is it that simple?

MAUD
She's always been the opposite of dutiful and Dad's never cared. So I can't stand to watch her suddenly pretend like—

EDITH
Because you've always been dutiful—

MAUD
Painfully so.

EDITH
It's never really seemed right to me—

MAUD
The difference in the way he treats Clara and I?

EDITH
Maud: I know you have feelings for Theo.

MAUD
Excuse me?

EDITH
I don't think he's right for you.

MAUD
Edith—

EDITH
I always suspected that you cared for him. Years ago I even suspected the two of you might have been fooling around—maybe you did; I don't need to know—but…I don't know; I saw it in your eyes last night—

MAUD
　Are you upset?

EDITH
　No, I'm not upset. I just don't think it'd be good for either of you to pursue something.

MAUD
　I'm engaged.

EDITH
　Clara told me.

MAUD
　Ugh.

EDITH
　You don't seem very sure about it.

MAUD
　I'm getting there.

EDITH
　Are you?

MAUD
　I want people to take my choices seriously.

EDITH
　Then you need to take them seriously.

MAUD
　I like Marco's family. They're exceedingly normal—

EDITH
　Right—

MAUD
　Disquietingly normal—

EDITH
　Do you actually know what you want?

MAUD
　I think I encounter myself in everyone I meet. I think I'm just too empathetic. I love Marco. But I could love someone else just as easily. It's almost too easy for me. It makes choosing someone seem so incredibly arbitrary.

EDITH
Because choosing someone is incredibly arbitrary.

MAUD
I can't get over it.

EDITH
You're not supposed to get over it.

MAUD
What are you supposed to do?

EDITH
You have learn to tune out the doubt.

MAUD
But doubt is the only signal I get.

EDITH
Then get a better radio.

MAUD
There's something cunning, or like, strategic about you Edith.

EDITH
I know my perspective might seem a little defeatist to you—

MAUD
No, it's not that.

EDITH
What are you referring to then?

MAUD
I don't know. I just feel like I saw you, in a flash.

EDITH
That's a little disturbing.

MAUD
I think my Dad likes women who can replace the imagination he never had.

EDITH
Who people are is a matter of interpretation, like evidence in court.

MAUD
You know more about Theo then you're letting on.

EDITH
Yes.

MAUD
You know more about everything that happens in this house.

EDITH
Sure.

MAUD
And you pretend like you're oblivious—

EDITH
I don't pretend: in a way, I become oblivious.

MAUD
That's pretending.

EDITH
It's survival.

MAUD
Is that what survival entails? Sleights of hand—

EDITH
It means listening more and saying less.

MAUD
That's such a domesticated philosophy of life.

EDITH
I live in a domestic space—

MAUD
What do you know about Theo and me?

EDITH
There's no reason to be nervous.

MAUD
Unless you have an x-ray of my brain, I don't see how you can say that.

EDITH
Never mind.

MAUD
No, I know you're not going to tell my Dad or Clara because I mean, you would have already, but—

EDITH
But what—

MAUD
It just makes me nervous.

EDITH
I shouldn't have said anything.

MAUD
I'm glad you did.

EDITH
Honey, your hand is shaking.

MAUD
Is it?

EDITH
A little.

MAUD
Oh, I see.

EDITH
It's ok.

MAUD
I wanna jump out of my skin.

EDITH
It's ok.

MAUD
I'm so fucking naive.

EDITH
You're not naive.

MAUD
Is my hand still shaking?

EDITH
Yes.

MAUD
Crap.

Lights down.

ACT II
SCENE 3

Night.

Clara and Doug sit at the table with a bottle of wine open between them.

CLARA
What exactly did the hospital say?

DOUG
His breathing is labored. His temperature is low.

CLARA
Are we gonna go?

DOUG
Have you looked outside?

CLARA
I thought maybe dying people get a free miracle before they die.

DOUG
It wouldn't be a miracle if we were able to drive to the hospital. Trust me.

CLARA
Honestly, I've never understood why I'm supposed to hate Pop-Pop. He always seemed alright to me. He seemed so peaceful this afternoon. He almost seemed wise.

DOUG
I'm not sure if you understand what it was like growing up with him.

CLARA
I think you want to believe that these inexpressible griefs are ennobling, Dad, but I think they're just crippling.

DOUG
Yo, kid—

CLARA
Sorry.

DOUG
I'm not sure why everyone's picking on me on today of all days.

CLARA
I pick on everyone, to be fair.

DOUG
Speaking of you picking on everyone: where's Maud?

CLARA
She's watching a movie upstairs.

DOUG
What about Theo?

CLARA
He's in his room reading. He asked everyone very politely not to fucking disturb him.

DOUG
Smart guy.

CLARA
He really understands the correlation between human interaction and misery in this house.

DOUG
I met Marco and Maud for lunch in the city last week—

CLARA
Pour me another glass—

DOUG
Is there anyone you approve of Clara?

CLARA
Not really.

DOUG
I'm trying to be optimistic about this guy—

CLARA
I'm trying to be real.

DOUG
You know, I love you so much Clara—

CLARA
Please God: no more sentimentality.

DOUG
Everybody finds me unbearable today.

CLARA
Yeah, it's a thing.

DOUG
I can't find support anywhere.

CLARA
And so you become your own Christ, crucified on exaggerated hopes.

DOUG
Um.

CLARA
I get ornery when I don't have a working phone.

DOUG
I know it sucks being stuck in a snowstorm with your family; but we all see each other so seldom…

CLARA
When you actually get family-time, all you do is preach about the value of family-time—

DOUG
Tell me: what would you like to talk about, Clara?

CLARA
Anything other than our our warmed-over family saga. Like, come on Dad, there's something thoughtless and arrogant about being alone in the room with just your own problems as a companion. I'm so tired of it. Why do you think I take baths all day? Because then I can just be by myself and not think about anything, if I'm lucky enough not to be bothered by anyone; which I rarely am.

DOUG
I hear you.

CLARA
Do you?

DOUG
Yes.

CLARA
I know how to spin words into the air; and I'm skillful at understanding the orchestration, but the actual melodies are a gift of the universe; in other words, I just say crap Dad—don't look so concerned and hurt.

DOUG
You have an awful lot of rules about how I should interact with you.

CLARA
I'm sorry!

DOUG
Your mother—

CLARA
NO!

DOUG
Fine.

CLARA
I refuse to let myself be plunged into the same emotionally claustrophobic fog that you and Maud have been wandering around in for the last decade or so.

DOUG
The word "mother" does not imply...

CLARA
I said no—

DOUG
You wanna talk about emotional atmospheres? Huh? How about you not being so fucking cold to the people around you for a change?

CLARA
Cold isn't the right word: brutal is the word you want.

DOUG
Ok that—that—how about you stop being so brutal?—

CLARA
It's an interesting practice to harness what's actually going on in your head and try to make other people feel it.

DOUG
Just say it, then; say what you're feeling—

CLARA
You should know already; because like—Dad—you have a profoundly profoundly feminine soul; I mean, you've lived this very gender and culture appropriate life, but really inside, you're soft and giving and want to be caressed. A part of you is still in shock that you had this like, gonzo-capitalist father who was vice-president of a bank and drank a lot and wore tailored suits and expensive cologne and had memories from the war and so on; you can't believe you fell into the role of his son, but you've never been able to walk off stage and yank down the curtain either; so now that the curtain's falling of its own accord, you're freaked out; not because of grief or even anger—but out of utter confusion.... I mean, where do you think Maud got the idea that growing up is about finding a man who will desire her, use her, punish her? She got it from you.

DOUG
Is that where the lecture ends?

CLARA
My notes become illegible after 'she got it from you!'

DOUG
Fun.

CLARA
Did it hit home?

DOUG
I really just don't know what you expect me to say.

CLARA
A part you of you is like completely impermeable and impervious. You possess the like the most amazing psychological homeostasis.

DOUG
I'm not going to give you a reaction.

CLARA
I'm not testing your reflexes, I'm attempting to communicate.

DOUG
That's a hell of a way to communicate.

CLARA
You know I'm like addicted to dating apps? I just swipe constantly. It's crazy. When no one's around, my phone comes out, almost by magic; by itself. It's sick. It's so sick. Boys, girls. It doesn't matter. I just want. Or I feel like I want. I crave. It's hunger. Or it's just a habit. I've confused habit with hunger. Sick. I really make myself sick. So I'm lashing out, or something. I'm lashing in.

DOUG
Now you're making me worried—

CLARA
We're getting off-topic.

DOUG
What was the topic again?

CLARA
I think Pop-Pop was also a closet-case; one in a long line—which is why he was such an alcoholic, and probably why you are too—I mean, you might as well inherit his liquor cabinet after the funeral if Maud doesn't get to it first—

DOUG
That felt calculated.

CLARA
The snow's really going crazy out there. Do you have any weed in the house?

DOUG
Edith requested that I stop. She got fed up.

CLARA
I'm anxious.

DOUG
Maybe Theo has some.

CLARA
I'm afraid to bother him.

DOUG
Well then I can't help you. Sorry.

CLARA
Dad—

DOUG
What?

CLARA
It's funny—the day you got married to Edith, I had this image flash into my brain of you, with a wedding dress hiked over your shoulders, being fucked by a strap-on-wearing Edith. I almost burst out laughing during the "to have and to hold" part of the ceremony. The more I tried not to think about it, the funnier it became.

DOUG
You didn't want us to get married.

CLARA
Not really.

DOUG
I know it doesn't seem that way a lot of the time, but Edith and I are happy together.

CLARA
I really don't care either way. I'm getting a headache. I wish you had weed Dad.

DOUG
So do I.

CLARA
I don't get how my life can feel meaningless and stressful at the same time. Stress should mean something meaningful is at risk; but I don't feel like that's the case with me.

DOUG
I worry so much about you and your sister.

CLARA
You worry we're damaged goods—

DOUG
That's not what I mean.

CLARA
Yes it is.

DOUG
I want you to be happy.

CLARA
I'm not gonna be happy, that's not in the cards.

DOUG
Why not?

CLARA
The only way to bind up pain is with pain, love with love.

DOUG
I'm not sure what you mean.

CLARA
Neither am I.

DOUG
Have you talked to Theo much?

CLARA
A little, why?

DOUG
Just wondering.

CLARA
I don't really know Theo anymore and I'm not sure I want to.

DOUG
I get it.

CLARA
No, you don't get it.

DOUG
Ok, I don't get it then.

CLARA
Dad—

DOUG
What?

CLARA
Never mind.

DOUG
Ok.

CLARA
   The snow is like the embryo of a ghost.

DOUG
   I love you.

CLARA
   Dad...

   Enter Maud.

DOUG
   How was your movie?

MAUD
   It wasn't really a movie, I was watching some of Theo's old films.

CLARA
   How were they.

MAUD
   Surprisingly kind of good.

DOUG
   I'm going to bed.

MAUD
   Goodnight Papa. Love you.

DOUG
   Good night girls.

CLARA
   Night.

   Exit Doug.

MAUD
   I couldn't stop crying in the shower just now, and then the hot water ran out and I stayed in there, crying until my hands started turning blue—

CLARA
   Jesus. Why?

MAUD
   I don't know.

CLARA
Uh yeah. So.

MAUD
I don't know what's wrong me.

CLARA
It's so funny.

MAUD
I can't take this, I really can't.

CLARA
Take what?

MAUD
There's no privacy in this house.

CLARA
Oh shit. Fuck. Fuck.

MAUD
What?

CLARA
I just realized something.

MAUD
What are you talking about!

CLARA
Something just clicked into place for me. That's all.

MAUD
What!

CLARA
I don't wanna say it.

MAUD
Sure you do—

CLARA
Uh, no. Nope. No.

MAUD
Was it something Dad said?

CLARA
Not at all—

MAUD
Something I said?

CLARA
You didn't sleep last night did you?

MAUD
No.

CLARA
Why?

MAUD
I had a lot on my mind.

CLARA
Is that it?

MAUD
Yes, what else would there be?

CLARA
Did anything, like, happen to you?

MAUD
What could have possibly happened?

CLARA
You could have had a conversation—

MAUD
With whom—

CLARA
I can rule out myself—

MAUD
God, it's really snowing like crazy out there.

CLARA
I feel like the soundtrack to this storm is something really dissonant.

MAUD
Who would I have talked to Clara?

CLARA
My money's on Theo.

MAUD
I went straight to bed after mass. Why are you giving me that look?

CLARA
I don't believe you.

MAUD
Why are you implying I was with Theo?

CLARA
Because you were.

MAUD
Did he say something?

CLARA
No—he didn't...actually.

MAUD
Because if he did, he'd be lying.

CLARA
No he wouldn't.

MAUD
You can't assert that—

CLARA
I think I can.

MAUD
Explain—

CLARA
Context clues.

MAUD
What context clues?

CLARA
Tell me what you talked about—you and our step-brother.

MAUD
Nothing, because there was no conversation.

CLARA
  Maud…

MAUD
  End of story.

CLARA
  Are you serious?

MAUD
  Totally.

CLARA
  It's brilliant.

MAUD
  Excuse me?

CLARA
  It's like I've seen the light—

MAUD
  You're seeing things that aren't there.

CLARA
  I'm seeing exactly what's there.

MAUD
  It's not possible.

CLARA
  You're doing a really nice acting job, let me tell you—

MAUD
  Why do you care about what's true and false, anyway?

CLARA
  I don't, I just enjoy the intrigue.

MAUD
  Then why are you pressing me like this. When you could just drop it?

CLARA
  Because you care—

MAUD
  I don't understand.

CLARA
About you and Theo.

MAUD
I feel like you're suggesting something…

CLARA
Uhuh—

MAUD
This is so disquieting.

CLARA
It sure is.

MAUD
Just tell me whatever you're thinking, please—just telling me what you're basing your…your theory on.

CLARA
Myself.

MAUD
I don't get it!

CLARA
I'm extrapolating the way I behave with Theo to the way you behave with Theo.

MAUD
What are you trying to say?

CLARA
It's complicated.

MAUD
Tell me—

CLARA
You shouldn't marry Marco if you feel this way about him; about Theo.

MAUD
Holy fucking shit Clara—

CLARA
I'm right though.

MAUD
I'm not gonna dignify that with—

CLARA
There's no need to be so defensive.

MAUD
I'm not being defensive. You're just making shit up.

CLARA
Your commitment to the lie is admirable, though ultimately doomed.

MAUD
I love Marco.

CLARA
No you don't.

MAUD
I don't need to prove anything to you.

CLARA
But I can prove that you don't.

MAUD
How?

CLARA
I just have to say the magic words.

MAUD
Which are what?

CLARA
I suddenly have the feeling that Pop-Pop died.

MAUD
I need a drink.

CLARA
I really felt like a wave of energy pass through me.

MAUD
Fuck.

The house phone rings.

They both jump.

They hear Doug answer faintly off-stage.

MAUD
Oh my god.

CLARA
I told you.

MAUD
So what are the magic words?

CLARA
I'll tell you in a second.

MAUD
Dad's gonna come down in a minute, just tell me.

CLARA
Do you remember how I was really anxious about my phone drowning?

MAUD
Yeah…

CLARA
I wasn't texting my editor last night, I was texting Theo.

MAUD
But your phone said "Sarah Nicole"—

CLARA
Sarah Nicole is a codename.

MAUD
Oh my god.

CLARA
You see what I mean now?

MAUD
Oh my god.

CLARA
It's a big house.

MAUD
Oh my god.

CLARA
You slept alone last night, but I didn't.

MAUD
Oh my god.

CLARA
When we were in high-school, Theo would refuse to sleep in my bed for fear of getting caught. Or so he told me. It continued that way until after high-school. For awhile. In fact: right up until last night. Something had changed, he suddenly wanted to sleep in my bed. I didn't understand why. But now I do. You.

MAUD
Oh my god.

CLARA
Crazy, right?

MAUD
Oh my god.

CLARA
Does he make you stick your finger in his ass too?

MAUD
I can't breathe.

CLARA
I have to give him credit—

MAUD
Please stop talking. I feel like I'm gonna pass out.

Enter Doug.

DOUG
Pop-Pop's dead.

CLARA
We know.

DOUG
Maud, it's ok—

MAUD
I need some shoes.

DOUG
We're not going to hospital right now, I'm sorry.

MAUD
I need some shoes.

DOUG
Maud sit down.

MAUD
I'm gonna go find my shoes.

Exit Maud.

DOUG
Is she serious?

CLARA
I think I hear the car.

DOUG
Goddammit.

Exit Doug.

DOUG *(off-stage)*
Maud! Maud!

Lights.

www.ingramcontent.com/pod-product-compliance
Lightning Source LLC
LaVergne TN
LVHW041306080426
835510LV00009B/875